⋆⋆ ZI ⋆⋆

VIDEO GAME
DEVELOPER

The Look Up Series #2

ZI

VIDEO GAME DEVELOPER

Real Women in S.T.E.A.M.

Aubre Andrus

ADJECTIVE
ANIMAL
PUBLISHING

LOOK UP
SERIES

"FOR THE GIRLS WHO ALWAYS DREAM ABOUT WHAT THEY'LL BE ONE DAY." — AA

Published by Adjective Animal Publishing in Santa Monica, California.

Visit us online at adjectiveanimalpublishing.com.

Design: Alice Connew
Photography: Ariel Moore
Logos: Shay Merritté
Illustrations: Aubre Andrus

The material provided in this book is for the purpose of general information and education only. The author and the publisher make no representations or warranties, express or implied, about the accuracy, completeness, reliability, or suitability of the information, products, or services contained in this book. The author and the publisher disclaim liability for any harm arising from the use of information found in this book. Any use of this information is at your own risk.

Adjective Animal Publishing and The Look Up Series are not affiliated with other brand names, product names, or trademarks cited in this book.

Video game screenshots courtesy of Zi Li.

Library of Congress Cataloging-in-Publication Data is available upon request.

ISBN 9781639460052 (paperback)
ISBN 9781639460069 (hardcover)
ISBN 9781639460076 (e-book)

TABLE OF CONTENTS

CHAPTER 1
MEET ZI

⸎ GAME ON! ⸎

Hi, I'm Zi! (It's pronounced just like the letter "Z.") I'm a creator and an artist. I don't work with paint, clay, or pencils... I work with code!

As a video game developer, I use technology and art to express myself. I turn ideas into games that entertain people around the world.

Painting, sculpting, and drawing have been around for thousands of years. **But video games are a really new art form that still needs to be explored.** Video games didn't get popular until the 1970s. There are so many possibilities in gaming. It's only the beginning!

Video games are unique because you don't just sit and watch—**YOU PARTICIPATE**. Video games are interactive, and the player is in control. When the player does something, like hit a button, the game responds. My job as a video game developer is to decide what happens when a player hits that button. And why.

All games have rules and a goal, which is a path toward winning. But a video game is different from a game of soccer or a board game—that's because a video game is played on a screen. It's software!

Software is a list of instructions that tells a computer what to do. These instructions are written in code. Code is a special computer language that is based on math.

I know how to build software. Software can be programmed to run as a game on your phone, computer, or video game console. But this is just one step in the process of making a video game. I'm like an architect, which is someone who designs buildings. I can map out the plans, but I rely on other people to install the plumbing, build the walls, and choose pretty furniture.

Video games are a mix of code, art, music, sound, special effects, and more. There are people who specialize in each of these things. When we combine our talents and work together, we can make a video game!

GAMES FOR EVERYONE

People used to think that only kids and teens—mostly boys— played video games. But now it's been proven that people of all ages love video games. Women and girls really love video games, too. In fact, more than forty percent of gamers are female.

HOW IS MATH USED IN CODING?

I can make a video game character move using simple math concepts like addition and subtraction. Here's a glimpse into some code that I wrote using a computer language called C# (pronounced: C-sharp). Can you find the addition sign?

```
1    void Update()
2    {
3    Person.position += new Vector3(0,0,1);
4    }
```

The addition sign means this line of code will move the character forward. Now let me change the addition sign to a subtraction sign. Can you guess what that means?

```
1    void Update()
2    {
3    Person.position -= new Vector3(0,0,1);
4    }
```

Now the line of code will move the character backward. Pretty cool, huh?

Hint!
Check Line 3 for the addition sign (+) and subtraction sign (-)

✎ PLAY TO WIN ✎

Video games are for more than just fun. Video games can help kids learn about history, geography, or math. They can teach people a new language or a new skill like coding. They can even help us stay healthy, happy, and strong.

Games can make important but boring tasks more fun. When someone turns an everyday activity into a game by assigning points or competing with others, it's called gamifying. Some people gamify their health by keeping track of how many steps they take each day or how many glasses of water they drink.

Some classrooms use gamification, like when a teacher assigns points to each book a student has read. Once the student earns a certain number of points, they can get a reward. Gamification can also make virtual learning more exciting, like when students answer trivia questions during a lesson. Students have fun playing while teachers instantly see how well the students understand the subject.

Video games can also help a patient heal. After getting injured, someone

Can you think of a time that you turned a task or a chore into a game?

might have trouble lifting their arm to feed themselves. Raising a hand to touch a button over and over again can help them regain arm strength while having fun.

There is even a special video game a doctor can prescribe to a kid who needs help improving their attention span. It's a racing game that was created by brain scientists and video game developers. The challenges in the game exercise specific parts of a player's brain. So, even though it's a game, kids can boost their brain function while they play.

It really is incredible when you think of the many different ways gaming can be used in our lives. That's why I love video games so much!

ALL ABOUT ZI

→ CHINA

Dog or cat?
Chinchilla!

I'm from... southern China
But now I live in... Los Angeles, CA

Ocean or mountains?
Mountains!

Birthday: January 11
Siblings: I'm an only child
Pets: My chinchillas Big Gus, Goose, Piggy, and Fish

Summer or winter?
Summer

TV or movies?
Movies

Morning or evening?
Evening

Favorite Color: Light orange
Favorite Food: Fried eggs
Favorite Ice Cream Flavor: Choc Chip Cookie Dough

What is your favorite thing about yourself?

I like that I'm an independent person. I can hang out by myself and have fun. But it definitely took me a while to get to this point. I didn't always feel comfortable standing out or doing things on my own.

Who do you look up to?

Agatha Christie. She wrote many great detective novels back in the day and her stories are still popular today. I respect her a lot and hope that I can create something (like a video game) that is popular for years and years to come.

Is there a story behind your name?

My parents hoped that I would grow up to be dedicated and focused, so they named me Zi. It takes the first word from the Chinese expression 孜孜不倦, which means 'continuous concentrated effort.'

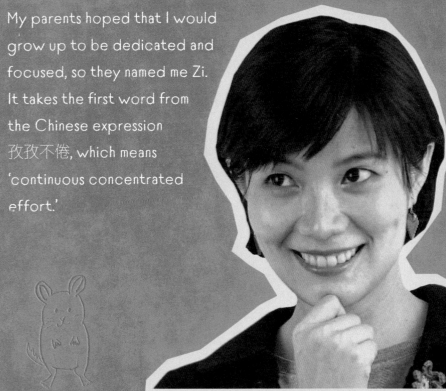

CHAPTER 2
HOW A VIDEO GAME GETS MADE

My friends and I won an award for a game we developed!

✐ START DREAMING ↩

If you're going to be a video game developer, you need a **REALLY BIG IMAGINATION**. That's because a video game can be inspired by literally anything. Inspiration is everywhere— from an image to a random thought to an experience.

There are so many different types of video games like puzzle games, action games, and role-playing games. (Turn to page 20 to see the whole list!) But I always want my game to tell a story—even if it's a very simple one. Stories make the player feel an emotion. What's most important to me is how I make a player feel.

Video games are a form of entertainment, which is an activity that people enjoy, like listening to music or reading a book. These activities make us feel different emotions. A song can make you feel happy, a rollercoaster can make you feel scared, and a video game can make you feel excited.

Can you think of a favorite book, song, ride, or game and how it made you feel?

My latest project is a puzzle-adventure game about a girl named Relu who explores an ancient world and discovers a magic crystal. Relu is chased by a giant shadow and is guided by mysterious spirits all while she searches for her long lost father. Players will experience wonder, adventure, fear, excitement, and more.

Once I've figured out the basic story, I can think about the really fun stuff: how will this game work? How will a player move through this world? What is the player's goal? This is what we call the **CORE GAME PLAY**.

We think about the **rules of the game** as well as the **actions a player can take**. In a race car game, the first player to cross the finish line wins the race. That's a rule. When players move the joystick to the left, the car veers toward the left. That's an action.

In Relu's game, players are rewarded with a piece of a map when they finish each level. That's a rule. The map will help guide Relu to her missing dad when it's complete. It's a mobile game, so players can take action by swiping the screen with one finger to move Relu forward, or two fingers to rotate the world.

Here's Relu and the magic crystal!

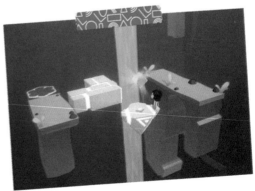

I write down all of these details in a design document, which is like a long report. It outlines everything about the game including the story, rules, goals, and actions. This document might change a lot while we make the game. But we'll use it every step of the way. It's our guide!

Here are some of the other fun details I think about when I create a game:

Levels: The 'chapters' of the game that players will have to work through before they can beat the game.

Rewards: When players do something correctly, they can earn new items, a new story, or a new challenge.

Camera angle: Video games aren't filmed with a real camera, but they have a point of view just like movies do.

FUN MONEY

Video game developers also have to decide what kind of 'economy' a game will have, which is whether or not a player can earn or buy things and how they will do that. For example, in a race car game's economy, players might earn a coin every time they win a race. Those coins could be used to buy a faster car.

ℓ INSIDE THE BOX ℓ

Before I let my imagination run too wild, I have to think about what limitations I have. Every video game has restrictions based on the software and the **hardware**, which is the device the game is played on.

VIDEO GAME PLATFORMS

MOBILE GAMES are simple games played on smartphones and tablets that are downloaded as apps.

PC GAMES are more complicated games played on a personal computer with a mouse, controller, or keyboard.

CONSOLE GAMES are played on home TVs with hardware, like a controller and a console, that connects to a TV.

HANDHELD GAMES have a controller and a screen that's built into a small device that fits in the player's hands.

PLAYER ONE

Video games can be single player (just one person) or multiplayer (two or more people). A multiplayer game can include other real-life players or the computer as an opponent. Multiplayer games are complicated and more expensive to make.

When creating a game, we ask ourselves, "Which device is this for?" and "What do its controls look like?" Every device has different controls. The controls tell us what kind of actions the players can take—and how the game can work.

When I create a game for a mobile device, the player's movements are limited to movements like taps, swipes, and pinches. There's only so many finger gestures a player can do on their phone. But when I create a console or computer game, I can assign actions to every button and joystick. I can even create combinations that lead to even more actions.

Here are just some of the actions players can take on a screen, controller, mouse, or keyboard:

Double tap	Swipe Right	Swing
Swipe Up	Push	Click
Swipe Down	Click and drag	Pinch
Press and Hold	Touch	Tilt
Tap	Swipe Left	Double click

VIDEO GAME GENRES

There are so many kinds of video games! Some video games are made up of more than one genre. Which of these categories is your favorite?

SANDBOX GAME

A player can wander around and explore an open-ended world.

ROLE-PLAYING GAME

A player becomes a character within the game and moves that character through different levels.

PUZZLE GAME

A player looks for patterns or creates a plan that will help solve a problem.

ACTION-ADVENTURE GAME

A player moves a character through a detailed story, which sometimes involves collecting items or solving puzzles.

RHYTHM GAME

A player moves to the beat with special controllers and accessories like a guitar-shaped controller or a touch-sensitive floor mat.

STRATEGY GAME

A player must overcome a challenge by carefully using the rules of the game to their advantage.

SPORTS GAME

A player moves an athlete (or a whole team) through a virtual sporting event like a soccer game or car race.

SIMULATION GAME

A player takes on a virtual challenge inspired by real life, like building a city or taking care of a pet.

EDUCATIONAL GAME

The goal of these games is to teach players something in a fun way.

EXPERIMENTAL GAME

These are games that don't fit into a category because they are so creative and unique.

ℰ IT'S GO TIME! ℳ

Once I have all the details written down in the design document, it's time to build a very basic version of the game, which is called a prototype. It doesn't have pretty art and music yet. It's mostly just simple shapes that show the core game play. This prototype helps us make final decisions about how we want the game to work step by step.

As we build out the prototype, we ask ourselves, "When a player comes to this screen, what happens next?" and "If a

player does this action, then what happens?" As we move along in the process, we have to get very specific.

Every item and action you see in a video game was designed and programmed by someone. We all work together to bring every idea to life. As a team, we create rules for the world of each video game. We follow those rules in every part of the game.

For example, let's say we want a character to walk into a room, open a book, and then jump inside the book. That sounds simple, but it involves so many things—and so many people! There are a lot of different ways a character can move. The artists and engineers have to **WORK TOGETHER** to decide how this series of actions will happen.

The art team will decide how tall the character is, how far it can step, and how high it can jump. They have to explain how their art will move and why it should move that way. The engineers make sure the software they've designed can do what the art team wants it to do.

From then on, that character will move the same way. Players will notice and remember how fast, far, and high that character can jump. Games must be consistent, so the player can quickly and easily learn how the world works. We make sure the player is never confused. **After all, the player is in charge of moving through the world we create.**

WHO DOES WHAT?

It takes a large team to build a video game. Video game designers plan the levels, characters, and stories. Game artists turn those ideas into digital art. Then video game programmers turn the actions and art into code using software the video game engineers built. Game producers manage the team and the timeline.

ℓ ART MEETS SCIENCE ℳ

In order to create the **IMAGINARY WORLD** of a video game, you have to understand how the real world works. Video games are pretend, but they have to be logical—that means they have to make sense! The video game world should follow the rules of our world like light, shadow, and gravity.

If I designed a video game about **horses**, the horse would gallop the same way a real horse would gallop. It would move faster than a human or any other two-legged character. When the horse jumped, a shadow would appear underneath it if the sun was shining overhead.

If I designed a video game about **flying unicorns**, the unicorn's wings would flap the same way a bird's wings do. The unicorn would land softly just like a bird does. So, video games are rooted in reality even if they have fantasy elements.

As we build out the video game, testers constantly play the game. **Video game testers get paid to play video games.** It's a real job! But it's not all fun. These testers may have to play one level over and over and over again. They compare the game to the design document to make sure every detail is correct. They also report any bugs or glitches they find.

A bug is an error. The game might crash, or shut down, or freeze in place. A glitch happens when something doesn't work the way it's supposed to—maybe the wrong image appears or the wrong music plays. **This happens when there is a mistake in the coding.** If the computer can't understand the instructions it was given, then it can't perform the correct task.

Sometimes we fix the code in one place, which causes a problem in another place. **IT'S LIKE A GIANT PUZZLE!** Even after a video game is finished, players might find bugs or glitches. If this happens, we'll update the game to fix the problem. So, in one sense, a video game is never done!

Inspiration is everywhere! I'm always looking for ideas for my next game.

FROM IDEA TO VIDEO GAME

1. We choose the device, the genre, and whether it's single or multiplayer. We also think about who will play this game and what ages it's for.

2. Then we ask ourselves: what is this game about? We create a story and a goal.

3. Next, we define the rules, economy, actions, and controls. We write everything down in a design document.

4. It's time to make a very simple prototype, which we call a gray box prototype. Our team tests it out to make sure all the core game play works.

5. The art team sketches characters and settings. The engineers make sure all of these ideas are possible, and the programmers begin coding.

8. The quality assurance team tests the game for bugs, which are flaws in the game. They compare the design document to the final video game.

9. We show the game to a small group of players for final testing. If any more bugs appear, we'll update the game to fix the problem.

7. Real players test the video game, which has now been programmed with art and sound. They have to keep it a secret because the game isn't out yet!

10. We're live! The game is available for everyone to play. Some really popular games get downloaded more than 1 billion times!

6. It's time for the sound. A composer creates the music and an actor records dialogue, which is what the characters are going to say.

FUN FACT!

A simple mobile game could be made in a few months but a more complex console game could take a few years.

CHAPTER 3
HOW DID I GET HERE?

This is my grandmother and me in China

manga

✐ SCHOOL DAYS ✐

You might be surprised to learn that I never played video games as a kid! I loved hanging out with my friends. We played **CAT'S CRADLE**, which is a string that you loop between your hands. You can make cool shapes by lacing your fingers through the strings in a certain way.

In school, I was always better at math than language arts. However, **I loved to read novels and manga**, which are Japanese comics. I wanted to be a part of the beautiful **FANTASY** worlds that were created within the pages of these books. That's how I first grew interested in storytelling and art.

I also collected cute erasers, pencils, and notebooks in pretty patterns and colors. I didn't realize it at the time, but this hobby of mine stemmed from **my love of design**. I liked how things looked and felt. Eventually, I joined an art club because I thought it would be cool to be a painter. I really enjoyed painting, and my parents were proud of my art.

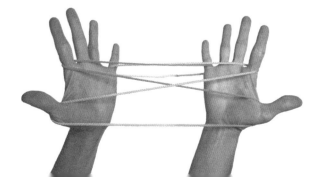

In China, school is very competitive. I studied a lot, and I was afraid that painting was taking time away from my studies. The other students weren't doing creative things on the side like I was. I didn't feel comfortable standing out, and I was sensitive about it. So, I decided to give up painting— even though it had been my favorite hobby for years.

Have you ever felt pressured to stop doing something you loved?

Because I studied hard, I did really well on the final exams in high school. That meant that it was easier for me to choose any kind of college or major that I wanted. I couldn't stop thinking about painting! I found a really cool major called Digital Media at a university in Beijing.

Here I am in high school with my friends!

Digital media combined art and technology, and it happened to be an engineering degree. Engineers solve problems with science and math. I loved science, math, and art, so it really was the perfect degree for me. I applied to the school and got in! I couldn't wait to get back into art.

Can you think of a time that you knew you were meant to do something?

OFF TO UNIVERSITY!

In Beijing, I loved my classes as well as the people I met. We were all engineering students who liked art. I could always find someone who I could relate to. In class, we learned the basics of digital art, programming, and math, and how they could be used in video games and movies.

As graduation got closer, I wasn't sure what I wanted to become. I could be an animator, which is an artist who draws images that move for movies or video games. Or I could become a video game developer, which is someone who builds and codes games. I decided to apply to a graduate school that could help me better figure out which career path I wanted to follow.

A few months later, I hopped on a plane headed to Los Angeles, California to earn an Interactive Media and Games degree at the University of Southern California. It was a Master of Fine Arts program, which is an advanced art degree. I would learn even more about gaming, and how to use technology to make art. I couldn't wait!

ZI'S UNIVERSITIES

School: Beijing University of Posts and Telecommunications
Location: Beijing, China
Major: Digital Media

School: University of Southern California
Location: Los Angeles, California
Major: Interactive Media and Games

FUN FACT!

USC is the #1 game design school in North America and has been since 2009, according to the Princeton Review.

GETTING SCHOOLED

Video game degrees didn't even exist until the 1990s! People who wanted to work in video games had to get degrees in software engineering or computer science. Now colleges around the world offer all different kinds of video game degrees.

Here I am graduating from USC with my friends!

✒ FINDING MY PLACE ✑

Moving to the United States was so EXCITING. But shortly after arriving, **I grew very homesick**. Everything was different. I understood English but couldn't keep up with what everyone was saying. The students ignored me. I was so upset at one point that I cried in class.

The other students had played video games their whole lives. Truthfully, I wasn't even really a gamer! I was an artist first. I decided to be proud of my differences. I created games based on my perspective, which is how I look at and experience the world. For example, I designed a game where players hear multiple languages and have to choose which one is English in order to move to the next level. It gave people an idea of **how hard it is to be an outsider** in a new place.

As I took more classes, I better understood how art, sound, story, and technology mixed together. Gaming started to feel like the right place for me. When I left my master's program, I felt much more confident as a video game developer. I told myself, *I can do this!*

WHAT IS A MASTER'S DEGREE?

Zi has a master's degree in Interactive Media and Games. Here's what that means and why she earned it.

After high school, people can choose to go to college to learn more about a specific career. It takes about four years to earn an undergraduate degree. Instead of applying for jobs after college, some people apply to master's programs at graduate schools. It takes an average of two years to earn a master's degree, but students walk away with even more skills and knowledge. A master's degree can help graduate students become an expert on a subject and decide on a career path.

What skills would you like to learn?

WHAT IS A JOB?

Zi's job is 'video game developer.'
Why do people like Zi have a job?

People work at a job in order to make money, which can be used to pay for a place to live, food, clothing, and fun things like travel and entertainment. Jobs give people a sense of purpose, or a reason to use their talents every day. Jobs can also make the world a better place by helping other people or by solving big problems. You can meet cool people and learn new things at a job.

Have you ever made money by doing a chore or task?

What are some careers that you can think of?

What kind of jobs do the people in your life have?

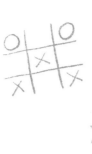

↑ mancala

CHAPTER 4
THE FUTURE OF GAMING

LEVEL
UP

RELUMINE

TECHNOLOGY TIME

The first video game, a simple tic-tac-toe game that could only be played on one computer, was created in 1952. Look how far gaming has come since then! Now we can play complex multiplayer games on tiny devices that we hold in our hands.

Here are just some of the other cool gaming technologies that developers are exploring:

Virtual reality (VR): A simulation that makes you feel like you are actually walking around a space and interacting with it.

Gesture controls: What if you could wave your hand and a character would move?

Facial recognition: A 3D scanner can memorize your face then create a character in the game that looks just like you.

Augmented reality (AR): This technology uses a phone's camera to place digital objects in the real world.

Wearable devices: Imagine a suit that could capture the movements of your whole body then make a character in the game move the same way.

Can you dream up a new technology that hasn't been invented yet?

Things move fast in the world of gaming. Sometimes people think a certain kind of technology will really make a splash—like virtual reality—but then it doesn't. And then something that people weren't as excited about—like mobile games—takes off and gets really popular.

No one ever really knows what the next big thing is going to be. That's why we need different voices to help us bring attention to different ideas. Sometimes, I'm the only female on my team at work. It would be easier for my voice to be heard if there were other people like me. But I don't see this as a sign of weakness. I just have to try harder to make sure my voice and opinions are heard.

For example, many games that are targeted toward boys are about action and fighting. And games that are targeted toward girls are about fashion, cooking, or caring for a pet. I think we can make games somewhere in the middle that everyone can enjoy. Luckily, the video game industry is growing every day, so there is plenty of room for new people and new ideas.

A REAL PROBLEM

When playing virtual reality games, players have to wear goggles that display a small screen. But it turns out that a lot of players get motion sickness. That's part of the reason why virtual reality isn't more popular. No one has fixed that problem yet!

‿ GAMER LIFE ‿

I may not have been a gamer as a kid, but now I spend all of my time playing and developing video games. I make games at work all day. Then I come home, play some games, and work on video game projects for the rest of the night—after taking care of my four chinchillas, of course!

As a creator, it's important for me to **make projects of my own** after work. That's why I started my own video game development company. One of my puzzle adventure games won an award for being **INNOVATIVE**, which means it is an unusual idea that has never been done before. In the game, everything has two shadows. This was a challenge for us to code. But we did it!

It was an out of-the-box idea, but people really liked it. There is so much possibility in digital art and gaming. That means you also have the chance to design a game that's unlike anything out there. **START DREAMING!**

My friend Gregory Chen created this drawing to help illustrate what an object with two shadows could look like.

ZI'S ADVICE
FOR YOUNG VIDEO GAME DEVELOPERS

GAMES ARE FOR EVERYONE.

Whether you want to create art or write code, there's a place for you in the video game industry. Maybe you just want to play games—not make them. That's ok, too!

GAMES CAN BE SIMPLE.

Games don't have to be complicated. If your idea has rules and a goal, it's a game. Start playing different types of games to learn what kind you like most.

BE WELL-ROUNDED.

Get excited about both the art and science behind video games. If you understand a little bit of everything, it will be easier to work with others—and you'll make better games.

MAKE FRIENDS.

You can't make a video game alone. You have to work with lots of different people from artists to engineers to sound designers. Those friends can help you build your ideas.

YOUR IDEAS MATTER.

Your unique interests and point of view make your ideas original and exciting. Someone out there will love the things you dream up.

CHAPTER 5
YOU CAN BE A VIDEO GAME DEVELOPER!

✑ DESIGN YOUR ✑ OWN VIDEO GAME

Game on! It's time to come up with your own video game idea. Fill out the following pages with words and drawings. Then, on page 52, you'll make a paper prototype of your game and test it out. Here's some inspiration that might help spark an idea.

Make a game based on a favorite memory or place.

Design a game that could help teach younger kids.

Dream up a mystery or puzzle that players must solve.

Create a game about a sport, hobby, or activity that you love.

Turn your favorite book or movie into a game.

Make a game that introduces yourself to someone.

Now, create a simple story behind this idea by sketching or writing in the six squares on the following page. It's a storyboard, which is like a comic-book version of your idea. It highlights all the main points of your story, like what your character wants in the beginning (the goal), the obstacles that will stop them from getting it in the middle, and how they win at the end.

Draw a picture of the main character, name them, and then write three traits that describe them. Will your video game also have an enemy character? A sidekick? A character who needs help?

Character 1: _____

_____

_____

_____

Character 2: _____

_____

_____

_____

Character 3: _____

_____

_____

_____

Now that you know what your video game is about, give it a catchy name.

Where will this video game take place? Mountains? Underwater? Desert? A made-up city? In the future or the past? Describe it in detail or draw the setting below.

Circle the words that best describe your video game.

adventure	sandbox	console game	exciting
puzzle	strategy	computer game	slow
educational	experimental	for kids 10+	fast
simulation	single player	for all ages	fun
sports	multiplayer	happy	challenging
role-playing	mobile game	scary	magical

Every game has rules. Write down the rules of your game. How does a player win the game? What are they working toward?

Now think about the actions a player can take. How will players use the controls to move through the world? What movements will your character make?

_____ **will** _____

[this control]   [make this action]

_____ **will** _____

[this control]   [make this action]

_____ **will** _____

[this control]   [make this action]

_____ **will** _____

[this control]   [make this action]

If your world has an economy, which is a way for players to earn or buy things, how does it work?

Draw what some of these items might look like, and how they will help your character win or move forward in the game.

Draw some rewards or items that your players can earn along the way, as well as what those objects do.

✒ MAP IT OUT ✒

Create a map of your game. It could look like a tabletop board game version or a more realistic view of the world from above. What sights and places will your character see and what obstacles will they face along the way?

In this game, an adventurer travels through the ocean, mountains, and jungle to collect missing treasures before pirates find them first.

Draw your map here.

ℓ PAPER PROTOTYPES ℓ

A lot of games start with paper prototypes. **You don't need to know how to code to work with paper!** The goal of a paper prototype isn't to recreate the entire game on paper. Instead, you'll create a sketch of an important moment in your game by drawing a specific scene or level onto paper. Then, you'll move paper characters through it. This experiment can help you decide what works and what doesn't.

YOU WILL NEED:

2 pieces of paper
Pencils or markers
Scissors

In this game, a bunny has to load as many carrots as she can into a wheelbarrow for her family's dinner—all before the farmer finds out!

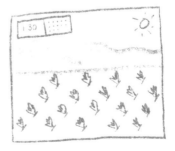

1 What will your game look like? Sketch a scene including the background art and the obstacles your character will face. Optional: You could tape a few pieces of paper together to create a longer level that your character can move through.

2 Then draw the characters and any objects that move onto a separate piece of paper. Cut out the characters and objects.

3 Now move the characters and objects through the paper world. Does your game work the way you thought it would?

You could also draw things that will appear on the sides of the screen like a countdown clock, a health bar, or a map.

PLAY TESTING

Explain the game idea to a friend or family member and ask them to try out your paper prototype. (If your game is for younger kids, ask a younger kid to try it out.) See if they can easily understand the rules and goal. Listen to their feedback, then use it to make your game idea even better!

CHAPTER 6
LOOK UP!

WHY WE LOOK UP TO ZI

SHE'S TOUGH.

Zi didn't let others hold her back from her dreams. She made a place for herself even when she felt left out.

SHE'S THOUGHTFUL.

Zi thinks deeply about how her art affects others, and how games can change the world.

SHE'S BRIGHT.

Whether it's art or engineering, Zi tackles every subject with curiosity.

SHE'S DEDICATED.

Zi wanted to learn everything she could about digital art and gaming, and she's devoted to learning more every day.

SHE'S ORIGINAL.

Zi forged her own path. She proudly embraced who she was then shared her creativity with the world.

What topics are you most curious about?

Talk about a time when you stood up for something you believed in.

List three things that make you original.

Give an example of a time when you didn't give up.

How has your art or creations made someone else happy?

Describe a time when you were proud to stand out from the crowd.

ℓ LOOK UP MORE! ℓ

There's so much more to learn. If any of the topics in this book inspired you, head to the library to find more information or ask an adult to help you search online. Here are some ideas to get you started.

CODING

Girls Who Code (**girlswhocode.com**) helps girls from third grade through twelfth grade learn how to build websites, video games, and more. Or, try out the largest free online coding community for kids, Scratch (**scratch.mit.edu**).

VIDEO GAME DESIGN

CodeREV (**coderevkids.com**) teaches classes for kids on video game development, 3D animation, virtual reality design, and more. Some classes focus on popular games like Minecraft or Roblox.

DIGITAL ART

Tate, a collection of British art museums in the United Kingdom, showcases cool art activities and games for kids (**www.tate.org.uk/kids**).

ABOUT THE EXPERT

Zi Li is an award-winning video game developer. She works with teams of engineers and artists to create exciting video game content. Some of the game titles Zi has contributed include Dissonance and Relumine. Zi grew up in Guangdong, China and came to the United States to attend the University of Southern California, where she received a Masters Degree in Interactive Media and Games. She currently lives in West Hollywood, California and founded Ammil Studio, where she continues to develop game experiences with creative imagination and technical programming. Visit her website at **liizii.com**.

ABOUT THE AUTHOR

Aubre Andrus is an award-winning children's book author with dozens of books published by American Girl, National Geographic Kids, Lonely Planet Kids, Disney, Scholastic, and more. Her titles encourage kids to be kind and be curious, and she is committed to writing books that empower girls and inspire them to become the leaders of tomorrow. Aubre received her degree in journalism and film from the University of Wisconsin. She currently lives in Los Angeles with her husband and daughter. Visit her website at **aubreandrus.com**.

WHO'S NEXT?

Meet Dr. Maya, a food scientist who believes ice cream can change the world. Maya does what she loves, which is traveling the globe, developing delicious flavors, and sharing her love of science with everyone.

Meet Amanda, a mechanical engineer at a toy company. As an engineer and a marathon runner, Amanda makes the impossible possible every day.

Parents and educators, visit **thelookupseries.com** to see who you can meet next and to find video interviews, free downloads, and more.

Made in the USA
Columbia, SC
13 October 2021

46968369R00035